MY BLUE CELLS

MY BLUE CELLS

Story Of A Man Beyond The Blue

Text and Illustrations Copyrights © 2022 by minnim

Published in the United States by BRIOblue

All rights reserved. No part of this publication may be reproduced, distributed, or transmitted in any form or by any means, including photocopying, recording, or other electronic or mechanical methods, without the prior written permission of the publisher, except in the case of brief quotations embodied in critical reviews and certain other noncommercial uses permitted by copyright law. For permission requests, contact the publisher below.

Brioblue Pictures, LLC

www.brioblue.com

Print ISBN: 979-8-218-07203-2

Ebook ISBN: 979-8-218-07204-9

1st edition, September 2022

MY BLUE CELLS

minnim

BRIOblue, LLC., Publishers

This book is dedicated with love

to all cancer patients,

survivors,

and their families

The blue-black bruises are in full bloom.

A blanched body and mind.

A deep blue soul lies within a purple within purple.

But at some point, I become a blue man.

I turn into such a savage blue man.

a Man aGONiZiNG

It hurts.

My whole body hurts.

It still hurts.

I'm going to be sick tomorrow.

I groan through the memories.

Was it near the pit of my stomach?

It was probably about a hand's length under it.

When was it? Where did it start?

I make a jumbled mess in my head,

But no answer comes.

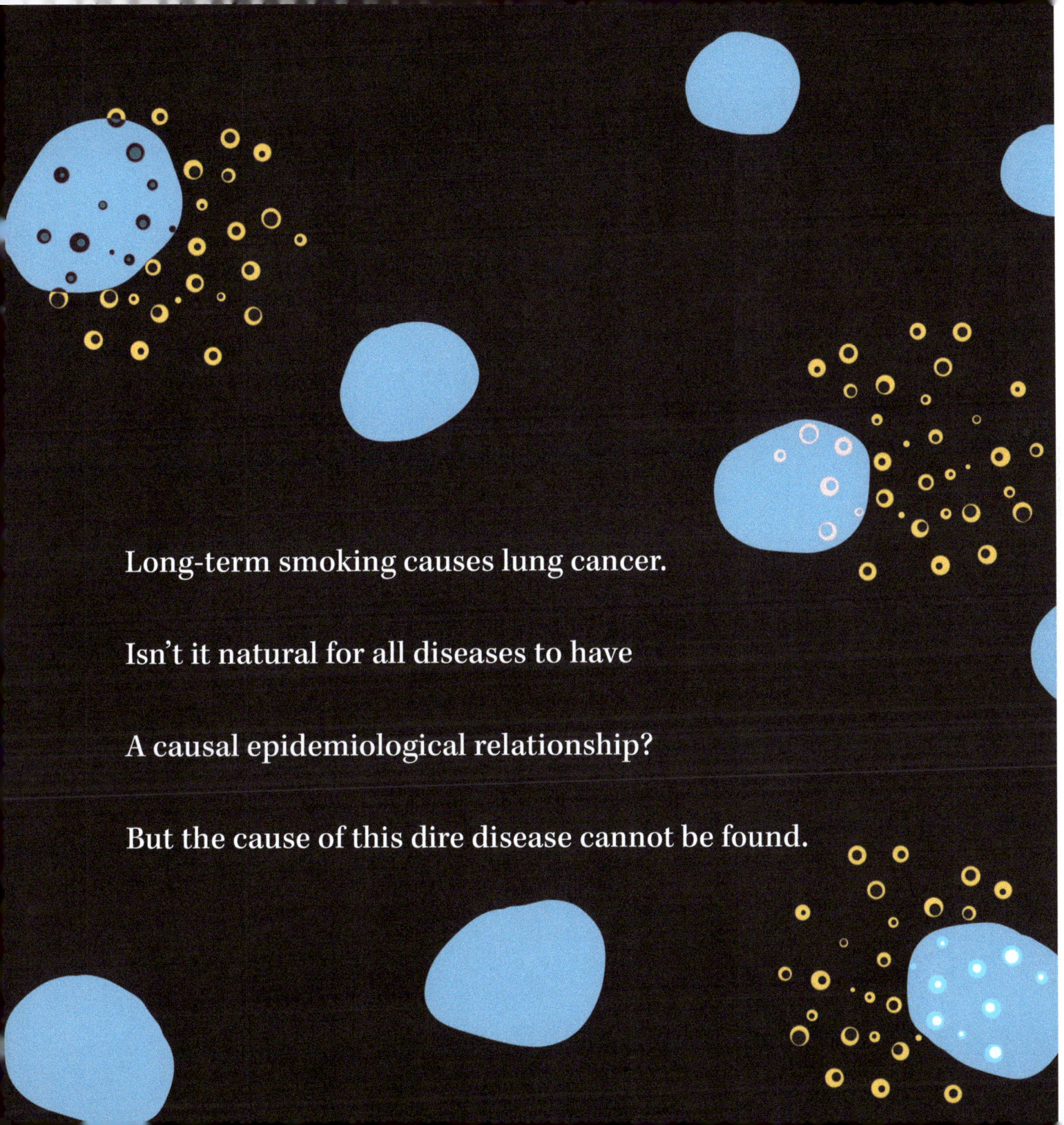

Long-term smoking causes lung cancer.

Isn't it natural for all diseases to have

A causal epidemiological relationship?

But the cause of this dire disease cannot be found.

Instead, a ball of fire rises in my throat.

It's a cry of resentment, distrust, anger, and hatred.

Blood mixed with regret and remorse.

Red rushes up over my tattered throat.

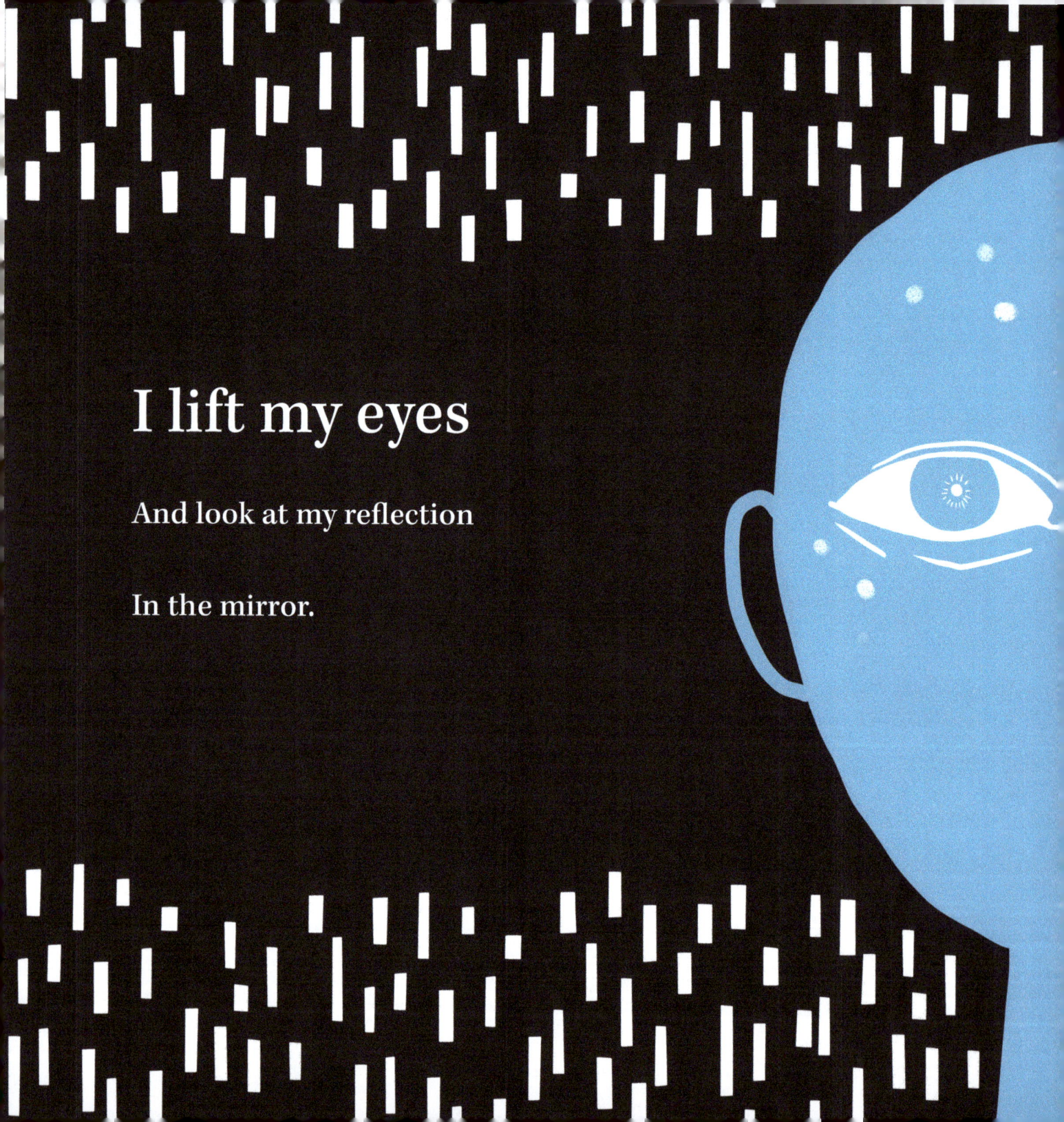

Who are you?

Because of my face,

Which is swelling up

Like a water balloon?

I look very unfamiliar today.

Especially.

a Man DRiFTiNG

Someone said:

Drifting without a goal is

The number-one reason

For failure.

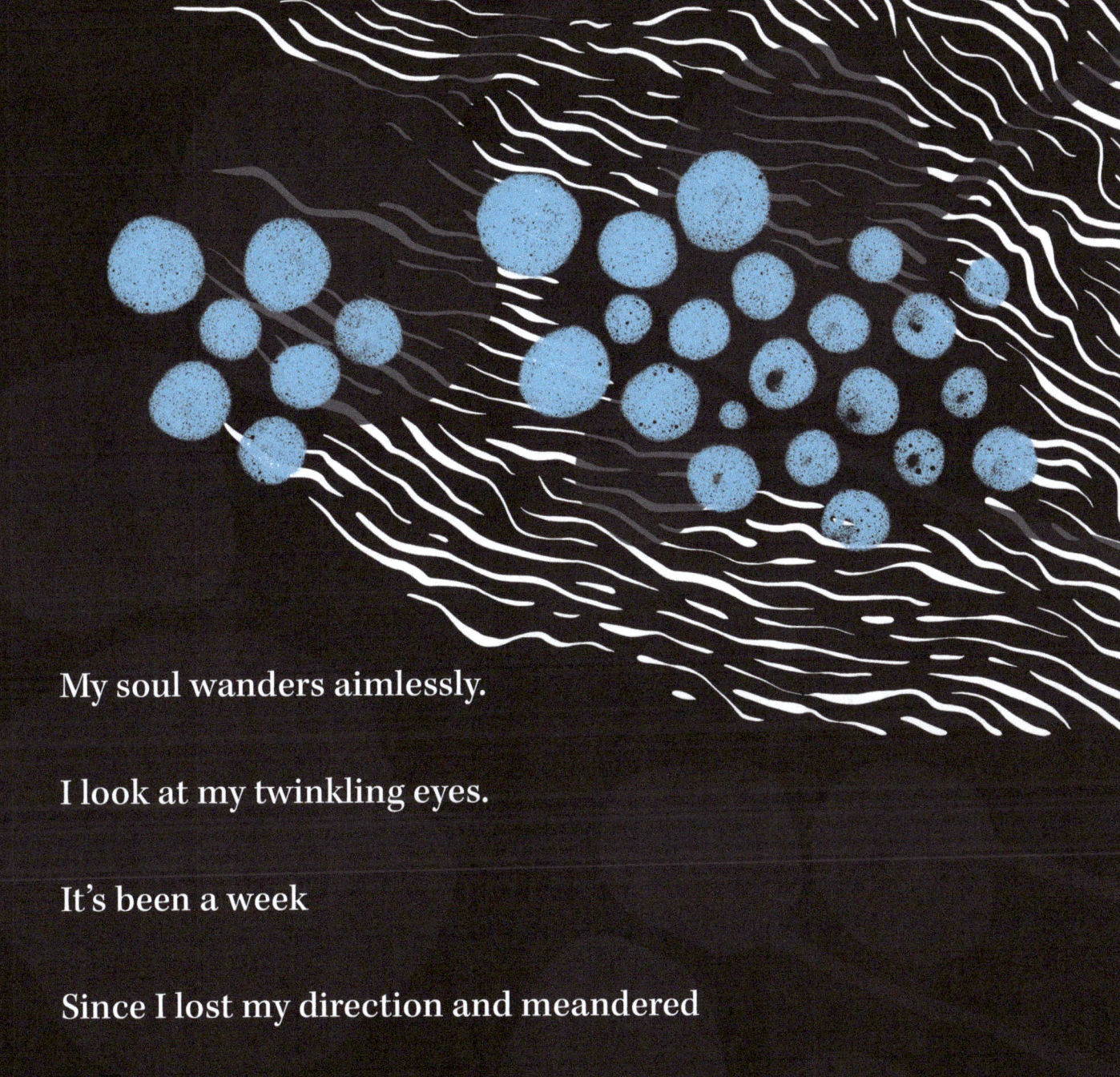

My soul wanders aimlessly.

I look at my twinkling eyes.

It's been a week

Since I lost my direction and meandered

Around day and night.

Because life, once held in my arms,

Exposes its sharp fangs and stabs itself into my chest.

Anguish is just a bonus.

The debt of life is worse than a hungry leech.

I got caught terribly in life's sweet lure.

I want to grip

The leech-like life's shapeless body,

Twisting it like a chicken's neck.

I'd like to ask it to pay its debt back instantly.

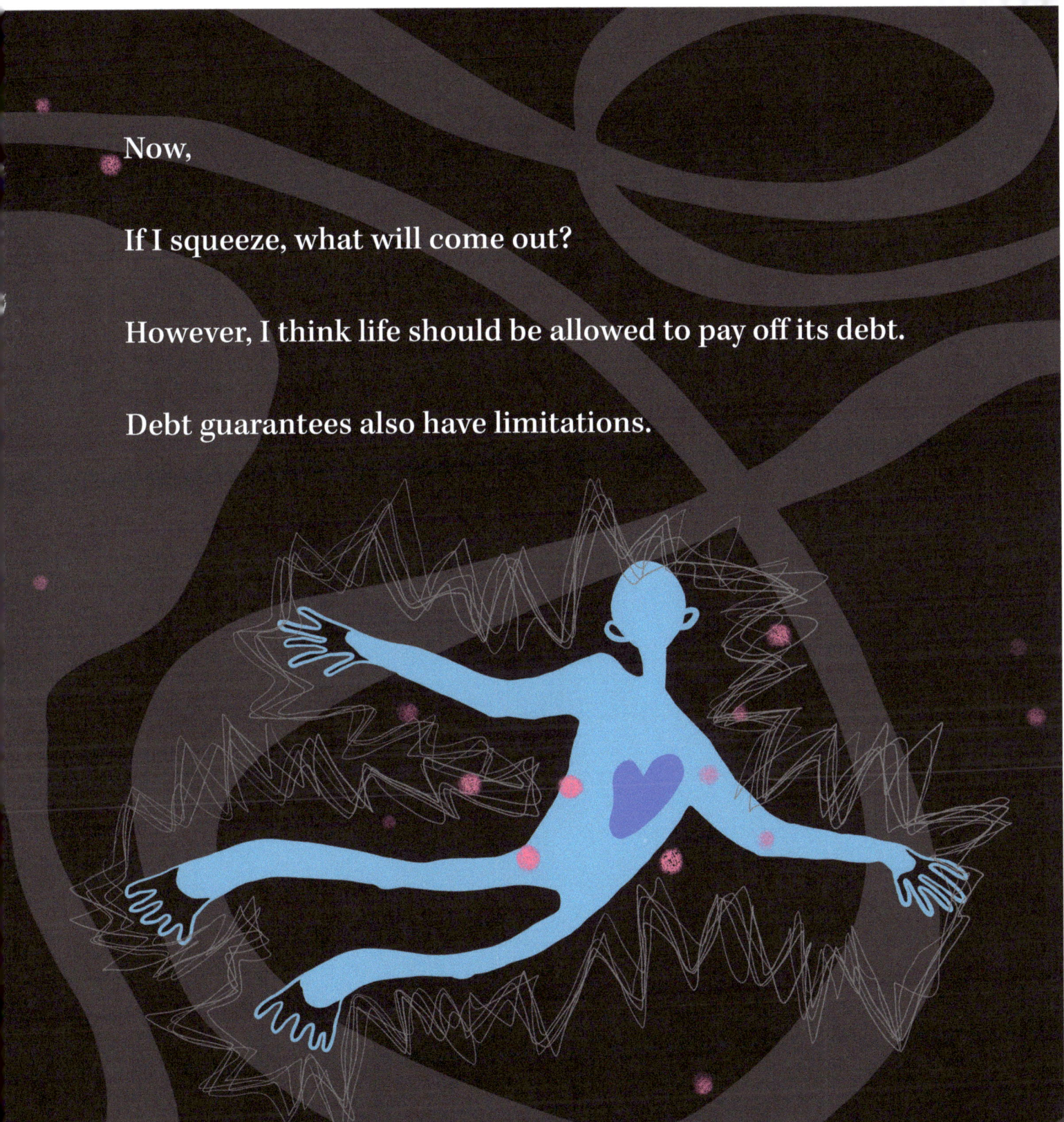

Now,

If I squeeze, what will come out?

However, I think life should be allowed to pay off its debt.

Debt guarantees also have limitations.

a MaN ReSiSTiNG

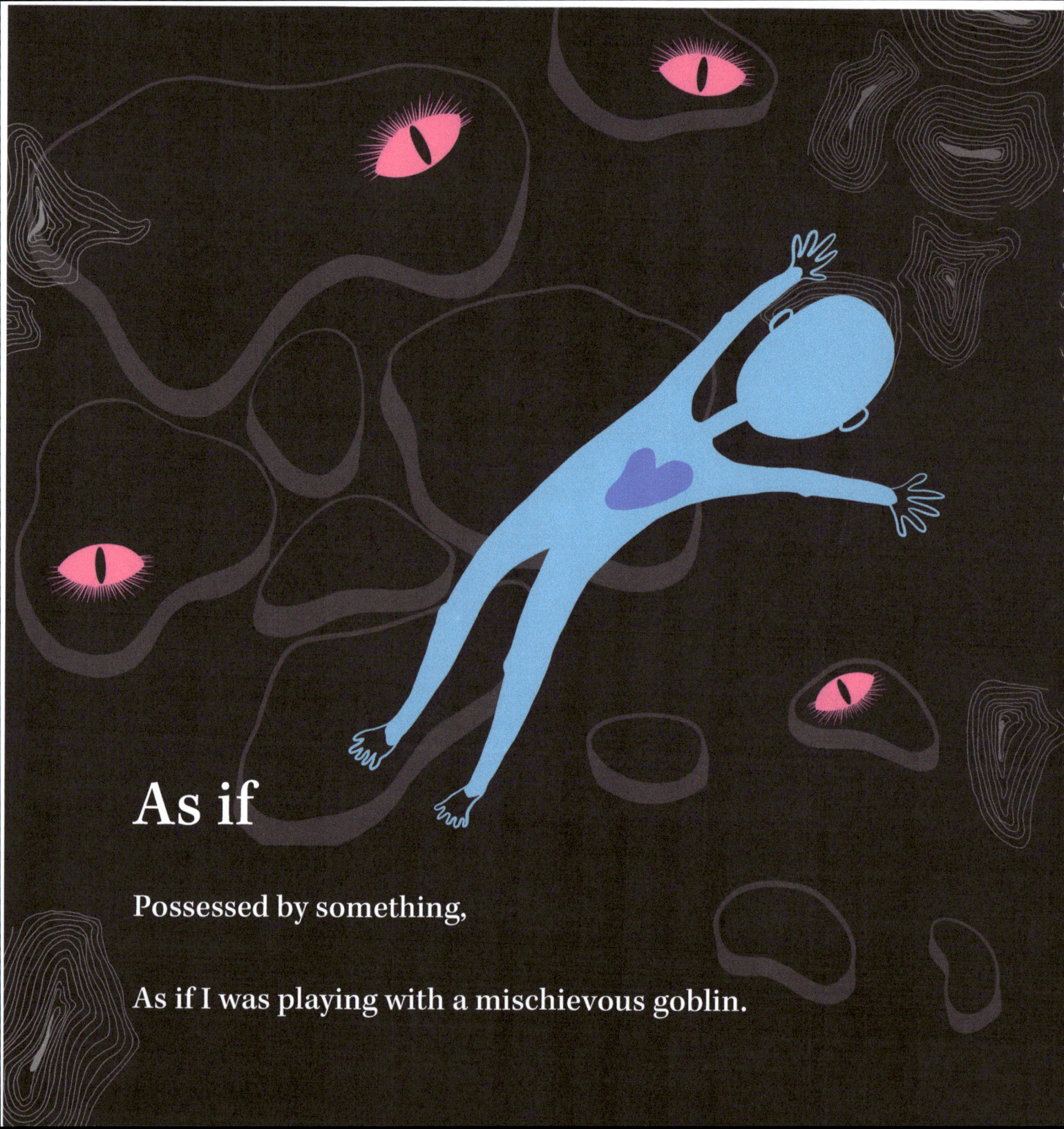

I couldn't come to my senses and be dazed for a while.

Curse it!

Like a fool!

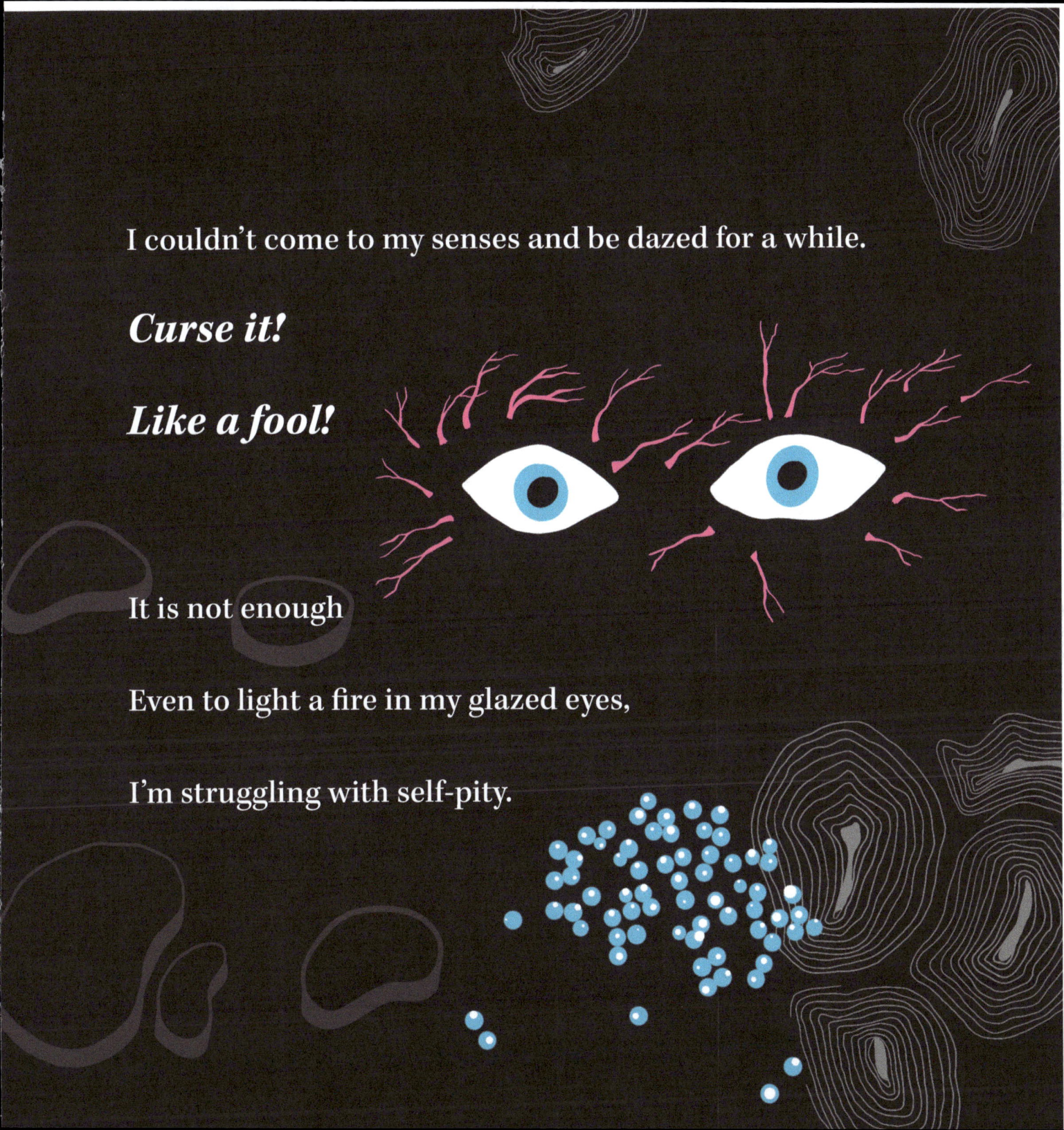

It is not enough

Even to light a fire in my glazed eyes,

I'm struggling with self-pity.

It feels like

I've been roaming a muddy road on the way to Hades,

And I've just stepped off the path.

Maybe because I neglected to make my usual affirmations

Every morning and night.

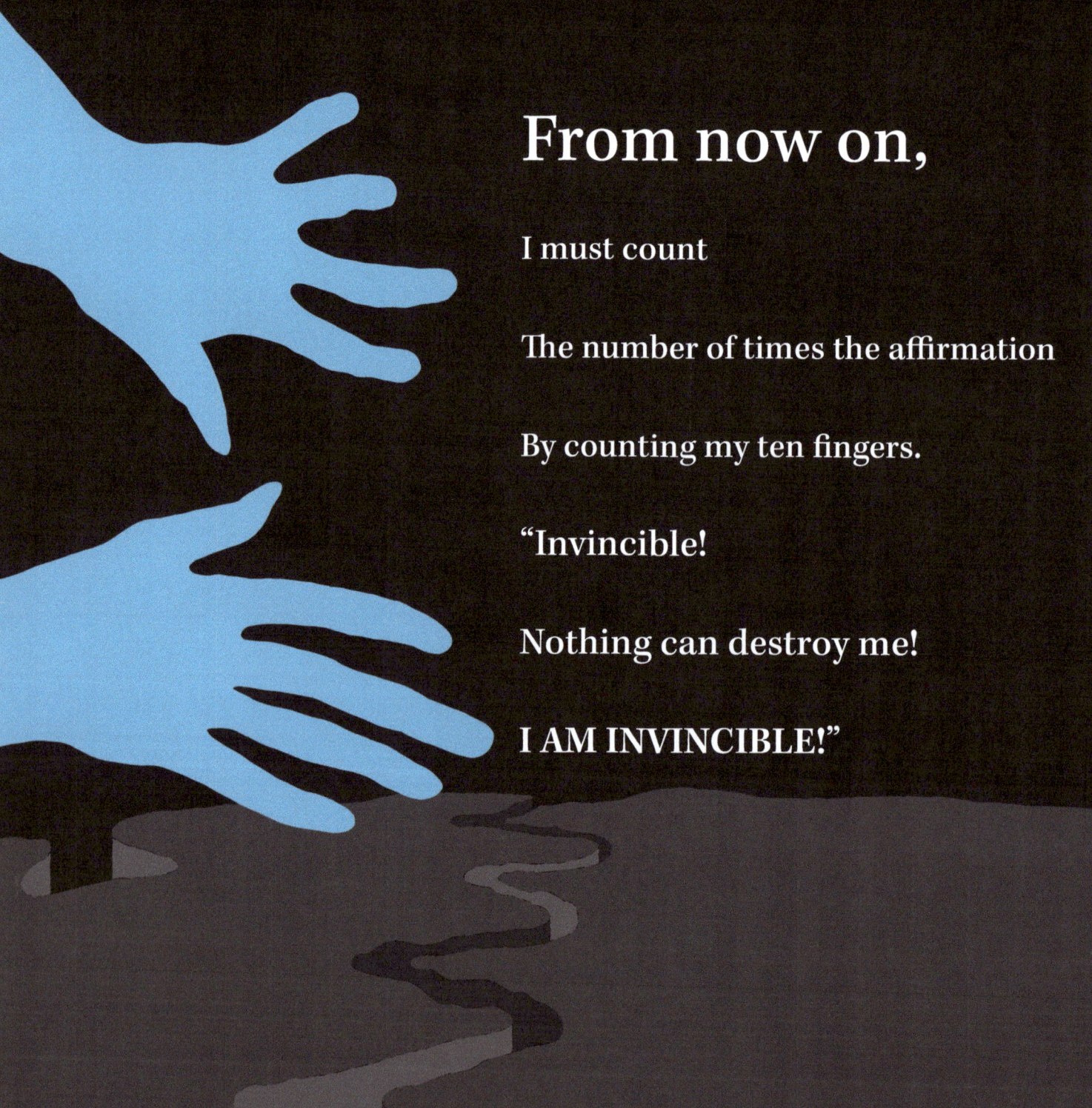

From now on,

I must count

The number of times the affirmation

By counting my ten fingers.

"Invincible!

Nothing can destroy me!

I AM INVINCIBLE!"

Even though

I have overcome many difficult and arduous hurdles,

It's hard to even imagine kneeling at this level.

I will fight.

I will fight fiercely!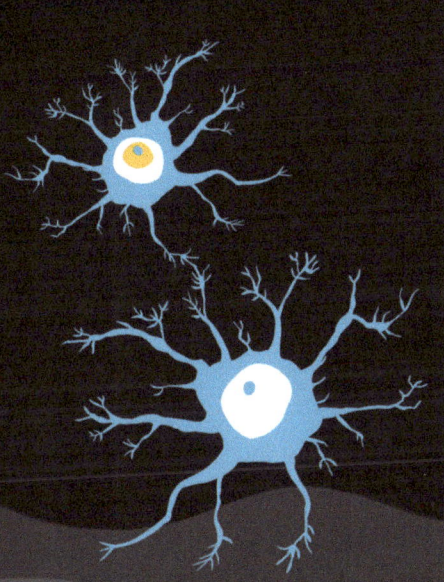

The scream of each parasitic cell in my body

Becomes an echo and punches my ears.

a MaN DReaMiNG

Whenever I opened my eyes,

Whenever my mind was clear,

Whenever my energy rose,

I would fight with all my power and intellect.

I'm so tired now

And don't even have the strength to lift a finger.

It feels like

All the energy sources that form me are exhausted

And in hell.

Is this what that means?

Puff, puff.

Even breathing in and breathing out is challenging.

Twinkling starlight

Pierces through my gaping eyelids.

The glistening eyes flicker in the macerated skin of inner lids.

One. Two. Three. Four...

They gather in the dark night sky and look down at me.

Each eye has the most immense compassion.

Each flickering eye greets me as a beam of light.

Grandma.

Grandpa.

Uncle.

And stray cat Dubu.

The glistening eyes flicker in the macerated skin of inner lids.

One. Two. Three. Four...

They gather in the dark night sky and look down at me.

Each eye has the most immense compassion.

Each flickering eye greets me as a beam of light.

Grandma.

Grandpa.

Uncle.

And stray cat Dubu.

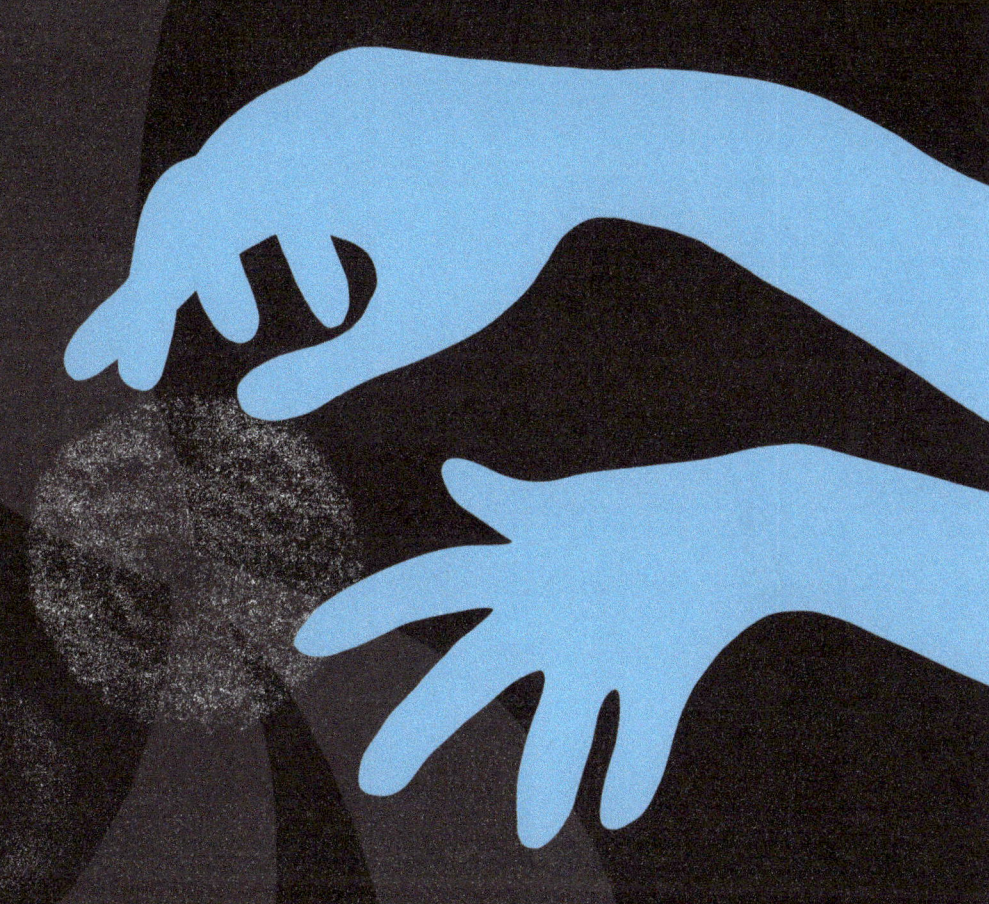

The breath of those who have already left me tickles my ears.

I gently close my eyes to the tenderness

That inches along my fingertips.

And I start to dream.

a Man SuRReNDeRiNG

White flag surrender.

A white towel was thrown over the ring.

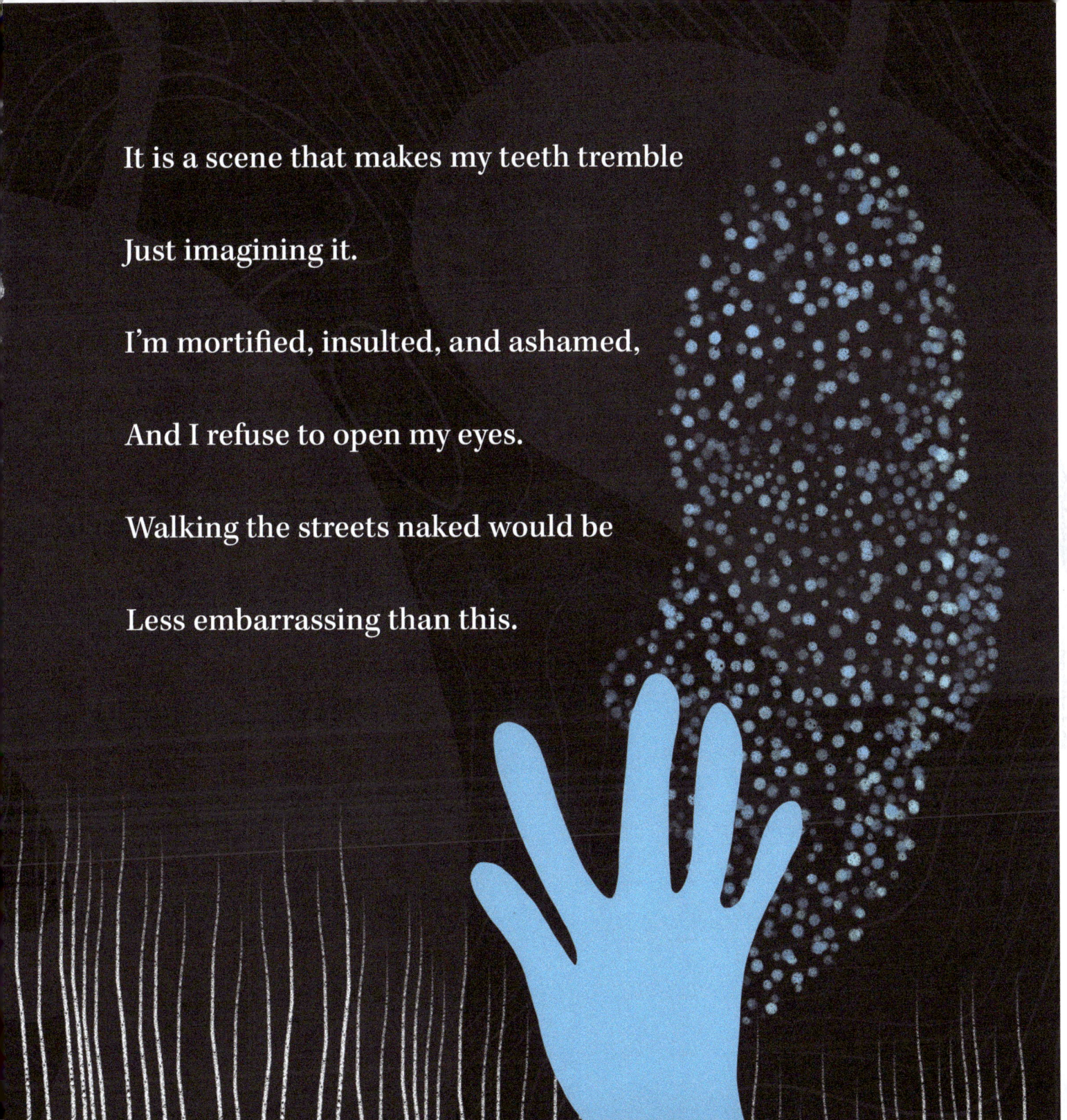

It is a scene that makes my teeth tremble

Just imagining it.

I'm mortified, insulted, and ashamed,

And I refuse to open my eyes.

Walking the streets naked would be

Less embarrassing than this.

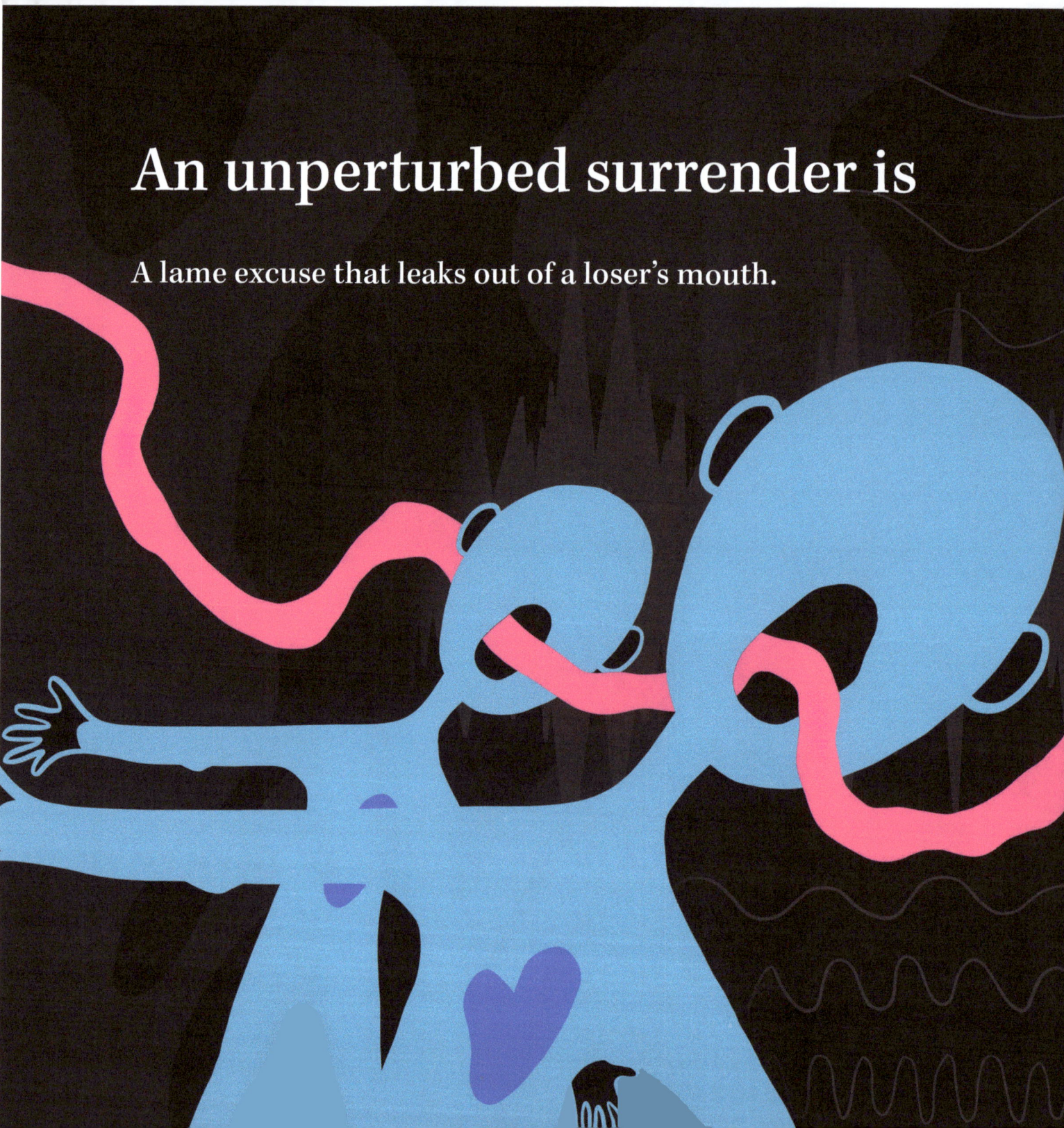

"Is that so?"

In no time,

An unfamiliar voice scratches the back of my head.

"Surrender is not about going against the flow of life;

It's about taking a step back."

At this absurd twaddle, I look around.

"Isn't it simple? But it's profound wisdom."

What are you?

What are you saying?

Hollow sleep talk is

Something you only hear when you dream.

This is not the condition now.

My mind is very keen and flashing fiercely.

It is quite unlike my limp body.

"Surrender itself is
Your perfect present.

The past ceases to have any power.

It's like bumbled dust."

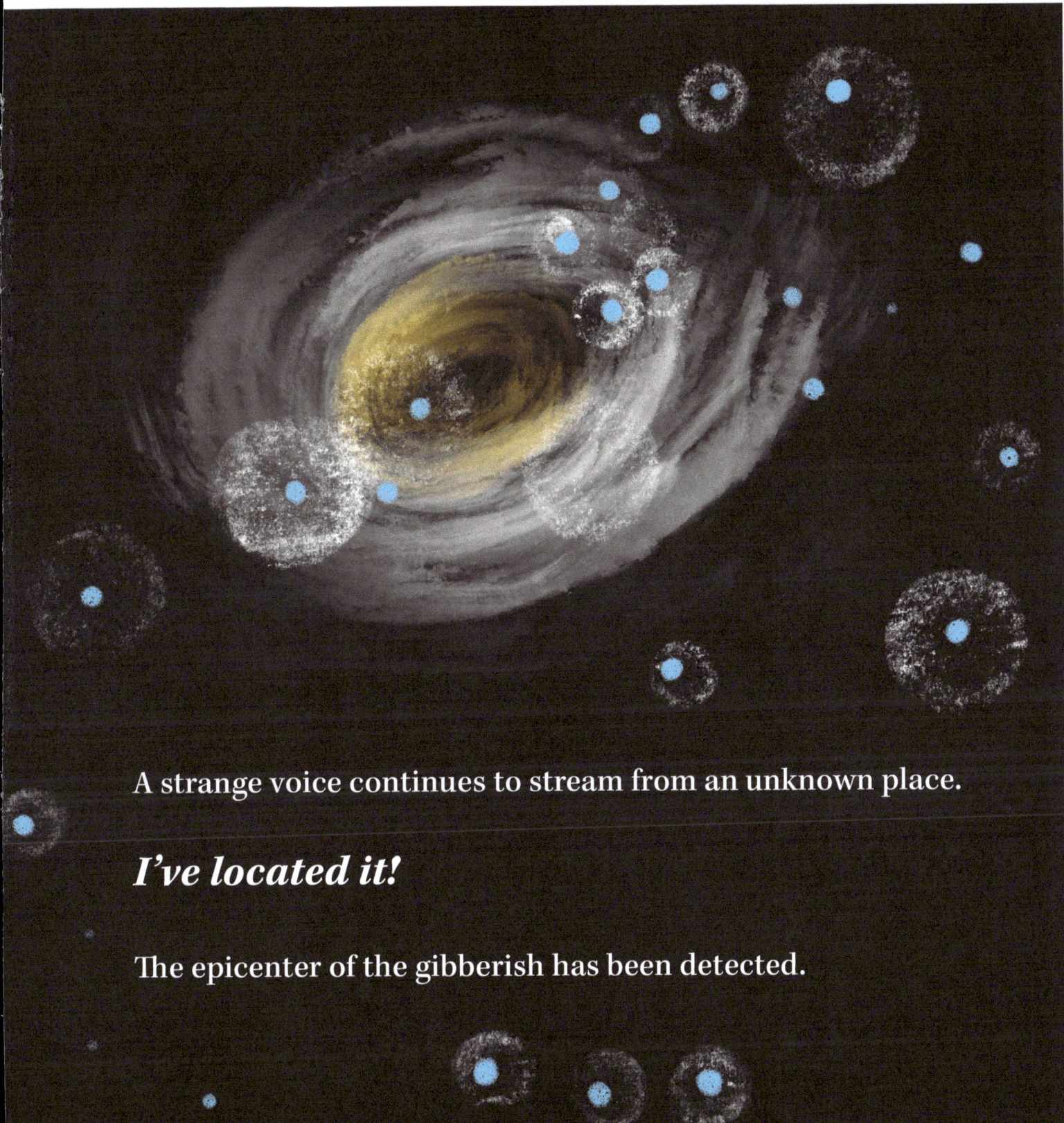

A strange voice continues to stream from an unknown place.

I've located it!

The epicenter of the gibberish has been detected.

...My deep-sea penetralia.

"Surrender.

That is the meaning of this presence

And the key to existence."

I mumble without realizing it as if I could hear it.

a Man Crossing

A shadow of light

Hangs in the gloomy darkness.

A ruffled shadow tail sways,

Whether it's playing a game of treasure hunting.

The shadow that casts a delicate scent on my cheeks,

On my shoulders,

On my chest,

And swiftly glides past my knees.

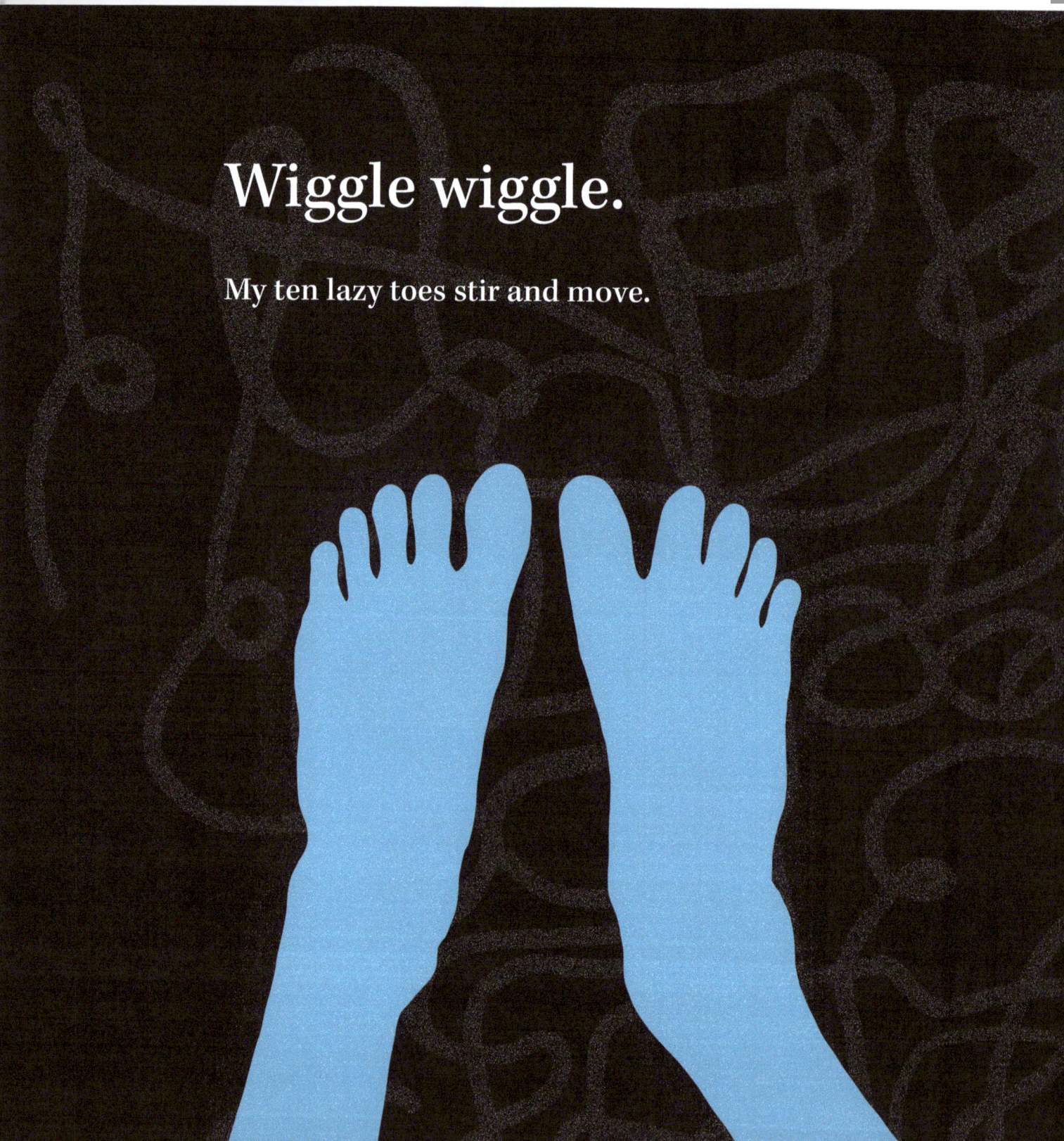

As if dancing,

As if drunk with a cheerful buzz,

Stamping to chase the shadow.

I stretch out my hand

Toward the fluttering shadow that splits the darkness.

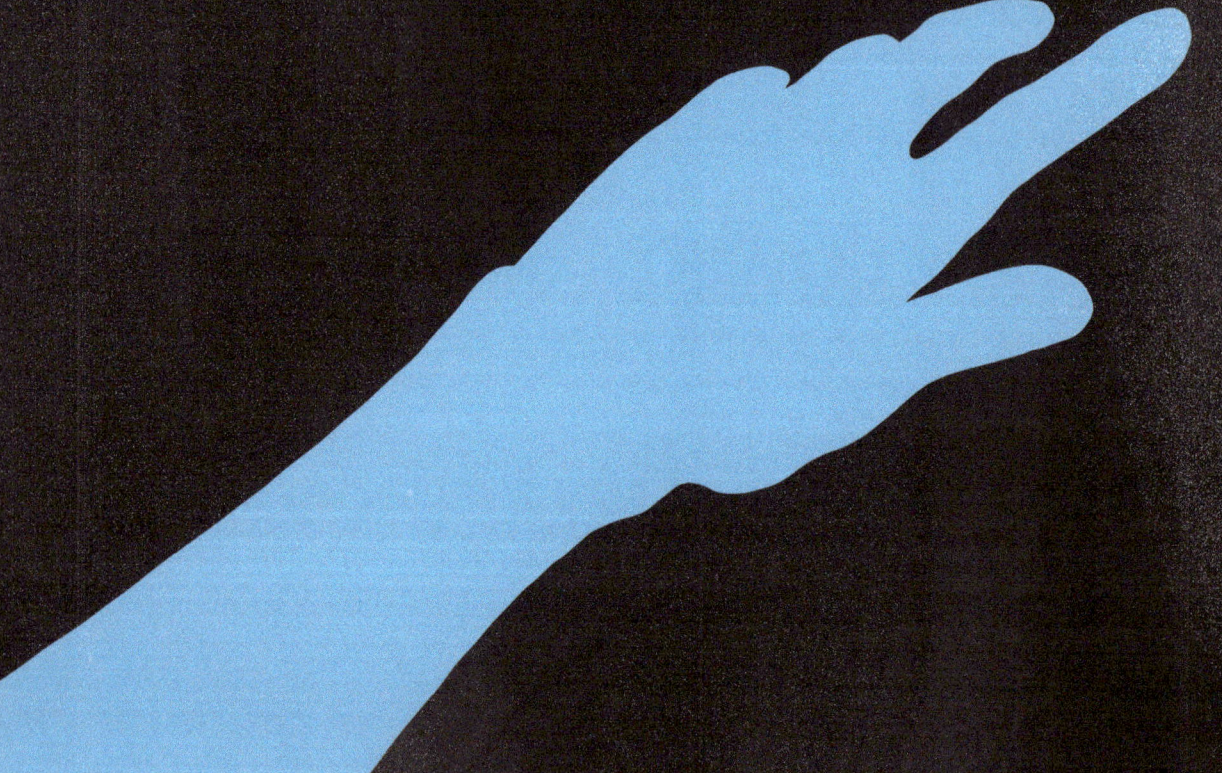

Like the sunlight seeping through a narrow crack,

My whole skin is colored brightly.

And I become the LIGHT.

I am no longer

A blue man.

I wave my hand.

The frivolous cells are already beyond the blue foothills.

Goodbye,

MY BLUE CELLS.

THE END

AFTERWORD

암. 癌. CANCER.

As everyone knows, cancer is a disease that occurs when cells ignore the death cycle and continue to proliferate. Eventually, the cells that should die and disappear. The problem is not only that these cells don't die but they also consume the body to keep living. Do they destroy the body to enjoy eternal life? This relationship can never coexist.

I found out later that the Chinese character 品 is a variant letter of 巖 (Chinese for "rock"). And also, Hippocrates named this disease Karkinos (Greek for "crab"). Does that mean a rock or crab is stuck in my body?

Because of these abominable selfish cells, I

lost my grandma,

lost my uncle,

and lost my beloved cat, Totoro.

And I also went on the operating table for cancer two years ago.

The fear of this disease was much more brutal and unpleasant than I had expected. Because these persistent cells are like crab shells or hard rocks, they can immediately crush my positive mindset.

One day, I decided not to fight against these greedy cells anymore. Instead, I decided to let them go. Then I started writing and drawing pictures every day, wishing the cells would depart from my body one by one.

I await the day when all our cancer cells are beyond the blue hills.

Yes, someday.

minnim

September, 2022

ACKNOWLEDGMENTS

My Blue Cells was a book with a slow-moving but progressive journey: It began as a simple drawing on my little iPad and eventually became a physical picture book.

This edition of *My Blue Cells* would not exist without the warm care and thoughtful encouragement from my doctors, nurses, and medical staff at Memorial Sloan-Kettering Cancer Center. Unfortunately, I was diagnosed with cancer during the COVID-19 pandemic, so I had to go through all the tests and treatment processes alone. As awful and scary as this sounds, my recovery phase was also lonely and pretty isolated because none of my family members could take care of me, since they all lived abroad. So now I have the perfect opportunity to thank my amazing doctors. Thank you, Dr. Alexandra Heerdt, Dr. Joseph Disa, and Dr. Jacqueline Bromberg. I thank Dr. Henry Hwangbo and the physical therapists at Broad Ave Pain and Rehab Center for giving me the strength to be creative and supporting me.

I thank my editor, Tracy Majka. Tracy, you're my dear friend, and it's an honor to have you by my side. Special thanks to my best friend, Seungah, for believing in me and my work. I also thank my loving friends, Andy, Catherine, Ji, Kevin, Ryan, Tom, and Vincent, for always cheering me up. I owe tremendous gratitude to my awesome friends, Ellen, John, Sharon, Jay, Wendy, Kay, and Evelyn. Thank you all for making me laugh and helping me heal so I can rise up and enjoy my life. Loud, long thanks to my family — Mom, Dad, Rose, Stan, and Meeyeon — for their love and emotional support. And one last thank-you to my husband, James: Without the iPad you gave me, and without your encouragement to draw, I would not have completed this book.

www.ingramcontent.com/pod-product-compliance
Lightning Source LLC
LaVergne TN
LVHW072117060526
838201LV00012B/261